Pepper Creatures

Make Your Own

Iryna Stepanova

Sergiy Kabachenko

FIREFLY BOOKS

Contents

Introduction

Archaeologists have determined that peppers, the fruit of the Capsicum genus of plants, which includes sweet bell peppers and spicy chili peppers, are ancient plants. We know that they were cultivated six thousand years ago on the plains of Mexico and Central America, and that by the time Christopher Columbus "discovered" America in the 15th century, the Aztecs were growing a variety of small and large varietals. Peppers quickly spread around the world and are now used in cookery, medicine, cosmetics, and more.

This is not surprising. As well as being delicious and versatile, the pepper is highly nutritious. More than 90 percent of a pepper is made up of water, and carbohydrates, proteins, cellulose, and mineral substances make up the remainder. It contains high amounts of potassium, fluorine and iodine, and except for garlic, peppers outstrip all vegetables in zinc content. Peppers provide more vitamin C than a strawberry and it is full of carotene (especially in yellow and red peppers), flavonoids, and small amounts of vitamins B1, B2, B6, and E. Like a multivitamin, but much tastier, peppers help to reduce hypotonia and to counteract various vitamin deficiencies.

Hot peppers, which are usually used as seasoning on savory dishes, provide more carbohydrates, proteins, vitamins and minerals than sweet peppers. Capsaicin, the alkaloid in chili peppers that gives them their pungency, stimulates the discharge of gastric juices and increases appetite. Hot pepper tinctures are used in the treatment of rheumatism, and can be used to counteract frostbite. Pepper-based cosmetics (balms, masks, creams) are used for losing weight, fighting cellulite and wrinkles, and for improvement of hair and nail growth. Peppers have even been credited with prolonging human life!

> The flesh and especially the seeds of hot peppers can burn the skin and eyes. Use gloves when handling, avoid touching your eyes, and wash hands thoroughly.

Dog 1

INGREDIENTS

2 oblong red peppers
1 pitted green olive
2 pitted black olives
1 chive stalk
1 small bunch of basil

1 Use one pepper for the head.

2 Detach two basil leaves from the bunch. These are the ears.

3 Place the ears on the head.

4 Cut a black olive in half lengthwise. These are the eyes.

4

5 Place the eyes on the head.

6 Cut the ends off the green olive. Cut the remaining middle section in half, without fully severing the two resulting rings. Unfold the halves.

7 Place the olive rings on the eyes. These are the pupils.

8 Attach the other black olive to the narrow end of the head. This is the nose.

9 Place the other pepper against the head. This is the body. Make two legs out of the chive stalk.

10 Cut one green olive end in half. These are the paws.

11 Attach the paws to the legs.

Goblin

INGREDIENTS

2 green peppers
1 oblong red pepper
1 pitted green olive
1 pitted black olive
2 round slices of leek
(from the bulb)
3 corn kernels
1 chive stalk
2 kidney beans
lettuce leaves

1 One green pepper is the head.

2 The two round slices of leek are the eyes.

3 Cut a black olive in half lengthwise. These are the pupils.

4 Place the pupils on the eyes. Lay them on the head. Use one corn kernel for the nose.

5 Cut the tip off of the red pepper. Then cut off a thin ring. This is the mouth.

6 Place the mouth on the head.

7 Arrange lettuce leaves under the head. This is the hair. Place the second green pepper next to the head. This is the body.

8 Cut two pieces of chive stalk for the arms. Use the corn kernels for the fists.

9 Cut a green olive in half lengthwise.

10 Place the halves against the body. These are the legs.

11 Lay one kidney bean at the end of each leg. These are the boots.

Lamb

INGREDIENTS

1 green pepper
1 oblong red pepper
2 pitted green olives
1 pitted black olive
2 leek rings (from the bulb)
1 chive stalk
2 kidney beans

1 Cut the green pepper in half lengthwise.

2 One half is the head. Place the two leek rings on the head. These are the eyes.

3 Cut two small rounds from a black olive. These are the pupils.

4 Place the pupils on the eyes. Use the kidney beans for the eyebrows.

5 Cut two short slices of chive and place on the head. These are the nostrils.

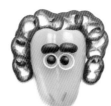

6 Cut the top off the red pepper. Cut the rest of the pepper into rings.

7 Lay out the pepper rings around the head.

8 Cut a green olive in half lengthwise. These are the ears.

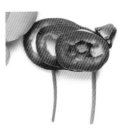

9 Lay the ears on the head. The other green olive is the mouth.

10 Place a large pepper ring next to the head. Lay out two more smaller rings as shown. This is the body.

11 Use the tip of the red pepper for the tail. Make legs from the remaining piece of chive stalk.

12 Cut a black olive ring in half. These are the hooves.

13 Attach the hooves to the legs.

Ali Baba

INGREDIENTS

1 green pepper
2 red oblong peppers
4 pitted green olives
1 pitted black olive
2 leek rings (from the bulb)
basil leaves
1 chive stalk
2 kidney beans

1 Cut a green pepper in half lengthwise, preserving the stem on one half.

2 The pepper half with the stem is the head. Use two green olives for the eyes. Place the eyes on the head.

3 Cut the tip off a red pepper, then slice the remainder into thin rings.

4 Stack some of these rings onto the head's stem in the form of a hat, layering from larger to smaller.

5 Cut two small, thin round slices from the black olive. These are the pupils.

6 Place the pupils on the eyes. Surround with the two leek rings. Use the tip of the red pepper for the nose.

7 Cut a green olive in half lengthwise. These are the ears.

8 Attach the ears to the head. Use two basil leaves for the moustache.

9 The other red pepper is the body. Use two pieces of chive for the arms and lay next to the body.

10 Cut a ring from a green olive.

11 Cut the ring in half. These are the hands.

12 Use two more pieces of chive for the legs. Attach the two kidney beans. These are the shoes.

13 You can also use differently-colored peppers for the body.

Bear

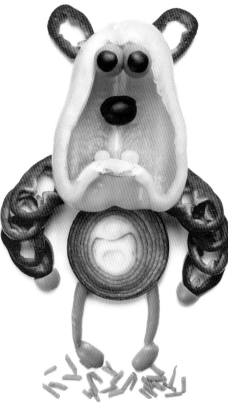

INGREDIENTS

1 green pepper
1 red oblong pepper
3 pitted green olives
2 pitted black olives
1 round slice of red onion
2 corn kernels
2 green beans

1 Cut the green pepper in half lengthwise. One of the halves is the head.

2 Remove seeds. Use green olives for the eyes.

3 Cut two thin rounds from a black olive. These are the pupils.

4 Place the pupils on the eyes. Use a whole black olive for the nose. The two corn kernels are the teeth.

5 Cut the red pepper into thin rings.

6 Put two identical rings under the head. These are the ears.

7 Place a pepper ring near the head. Place two overlapping rings on top. This is the arm.

8 Lay out the second arm, and use the onion slice for the body.

9 Cut a green olive in half lengthwise. Cut one half lengthwise again. Cut the other half horizontally. These are the paws.

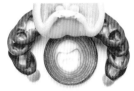

10 Attach the horizontal paws to the arms.

11 Use the two green beans for the legs. Attach the vertical paws to the legs.

Lion

INGREDIENTS

1 green pepper
1 red chili pepper
1 pitted green olive
2 pitted black olives
corn kernels

2 round slices of leek
  (from the bulb)
2 green beans
1 lettuce leaf

1 Cut the green pepper in half lengthwise.

2 One of the halves is the head. Make a horizontal incision in the bottom of one half. This is the mouth.

3 Insert corn kernels in the incision. These are the teeth.

4 Use the lettuce leaf for a mane and place the head on top.

5 Cut the green olive in half lengthwise, without fully severing the two halves.

6 Unfold the olive halves. These are the eyes. Cut a segment out of each to hold the pupils.

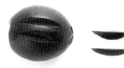

7 Cut two equal-sized segments from a black olive half. These are the pupils.

8 Insert the pupils in the eyes. Place the eyes on the head.

9 Use the second olive half for the nose. Use the leek slices for the ears.

10 The red chili pepper is the body.

11 Cut segments out of the middle of each green bean to create joints. These are the legs. Attach the legs to the body.

Cow

INGREDIENTS

2 green peppers
2 red chili peppers
1 pitted green olive
2 pitted black olives
2 round slices of leek
   (from the bulb)
2 kidney beans
4 chive stalks
1 arugula leaf
1 stalk dill

1 Cut one green pepper in half lengthwise. The half without the stem is the head.

2 Arrange the red chili peppers in the form of horns.

3 Place the head on top of the horns.

4 Cut two oval slices from the other green pepper. These are the ears.

5 Cut two round slices of leek. These are the eyes.

6 Place the ears under the head. Lay the eyes on top of the head.

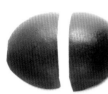

7 Cut half a black olive in two. These are the pupils.

8 Place the pupils on the eyes. Use dill stalks for the eyelashes.

9 Cut the tips off the green olive. Cut the remaining middle part into two rings. These are the nostrils.

10 Place the nostrils on the muzzle. This is the snout. Arrange the kidney beans under the muzzle for the mouth.

11 Place the second pepper half next to the head. This is the body. Use the chive stalks for the legs.

12 Cut the tip off the other black olive.

13 Cut the tip into quarters. These are the hooves.

14 Attach the hooves to the legs. Use the arugula leaf for the tail.

Bird

1 Cut one green pepper in half lengthwise. The half without the stem is the body.

2 Arrange the red chili peppers in the form of legs.

3 Place the body on top of the legs. Place basil leaves under the body on either side. These are the wings.

18

4 Cut off three oval slices from the other green pepper. One of these is the head. The other two are preforms the tail.

5 Cut the tip off the red pepper at an angle. This is the beak.

6 Lay the head under the body. Attach the beak to the head.

7 Cut a black olive half in two. These are the pupils. The two leek slices are the eyes.

8 Place the eyes on the head. Place the pupils on the eyes.

9 Arrange the tail.

10 Cut a ring from the red pepper and cut it in half.

11 Cut off an angled piece from each end of the pepper.

12 These are the claws. Place the claws on the legs.

Boy

INGREDIENTS

1 yellow pepper
2 red chili peppers
1 red pepper ring
1 oval piece of green pepper
1 pitted green olive
1 pitted black olive
2 round slices of leek (from the bulb)
2 kidney beans
1 chive stalk
1 lettuce leaf
10 corn kernels

1 Cut the yellow pepper in half lengthwise.

2 Remove the seeds. One of the halves is the head.

3 The two leek slices are the eyes. Place them on the head.

4 Cut half of the black olive in two. These are the pupils.

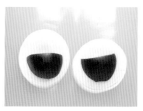

5 Place the pupils on the eyes.

6 Place the beans on the eyes. These are the eyelids. Use the chive stalk for the nose.

7 Cut the red pepper ring in half. From one half, shape a mouth.

8 Cut two rings from the green olive. These are the ears.

9 Place the ears next to the head.

10 Cut out the central part of the lettuce leaf as shown and arrange around the head in the form of a hairstyle.

11 Arrange the red chili peppers in the form of arms and legs as shown.

12 Place the oval slice of green pepper over the arms and legs. This is the body.

13 Arrange the corn kernels in the form of hands and fingers.

Piglet

INGREDIENTS

1 yellow pepper
1 red oblong pepper
4 pitted green olives
2 pitted black olives
2 round slices of leek
   (from the bulb)
2 basil leaves

1 Cut a yellow pepper in half lengthwise.

2 One of the halves is the head. Place the two basil leaves under the head. These are the ears.

3 The two leek slices are the eyes.

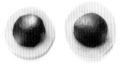

4 Cut two rings from a green olive.

5 Cut two small rounds from a black olive. Place these on the olive rings. These are the pupils.

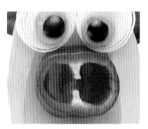

6 Place the pupils on the eyes. Place the eyes on the head.

7 Cut the tip off the red pepper. Cut off a 1 in. ring. This is the snout.

8 Lay the snout on the muzzle.

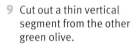

9 Cut out a thin vertical segment from the other green olive.

10 Place the olive on the muzzle. This is the mouth.

11 Place the other yellow pepper half next to the head. This is the body. Use two green olives for the legs.

12 Cut a black olive half in two. These are the hooves.

13 Place the hooves against the legs. Cut a tail out of a red pepper ring. Attach it to the body.

Parrot

INGREDIENTS

1 yellow pepper

1 red oblong pepper

1 pitted green olive

1 pitted black olive

2 round slices of leek
(from the bulb)

2 basil leaves

1 oval slice of green pepper

1 chive stalk

1 lettuce leaf

1 Cut a yellow pepper in half lengthwise. One of the halves is the head.

2 Cut the tip from the red pepper. This is the beak.

3 Place the beak on the head. Arrange the two leek slices as the eyes.

4 Cut two rings from the green olive.

5 Cut two small rounds from the black olive.

6 Place the rounds on the green olive rings. These are the pupils. Place the pupils on the eyes.

7 Use the lettuce leaf as the crest.

8 Use the green pepper slice as the body.

9 Place the body next to the head. Place basil leaves under the body on either side. These are the wings. Use two small pieces of chive for the legs.

10 Make claws from more small pieces of chive.

11 Cut a red pepper ring in half. Cut small triangles off each end, as shown. This is a tail feather.

12 Make two more tail feathers. Arrange these beside the body, as shown.

Turtle

INGREDIENTS

1 yellow pepper

1 narrow slice of red pepper

2 pitted green olives

1 oval slice of green pepper

1 pitted black olive

 **1** Cut the yellow pepper in half lengthwise.

2 One of the halves is the shell.

3 The green pepper slice is the head.

4 Cut two rings from a green olive. These are the eyes.

5 Cut two small rounds from the black olive. These are the pupils.

6 Place the pupils on the eyes. Place the eyes on the head.

7 Cut a red pepper ring in half. Cut small triangles off each end of one half.

8 Do the same for the second half. Place both halves on the head. These are the lips.

9 Place the shell against the head.

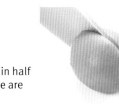

10 Cut a green olive in half lengthwise. These are the legs.

11 Place the legs under the shell.

Dog 2

INGREDIENTS

1 yellow pepper
1 oval slice of green pepper
1 light green long pepper
1 piece of red pepper
1 pitted green olive
1 pitted black olive
2 round slices of red onion
4 chive stalks
4 kidney beans

1 Cut a yellow pepper in half lengthwise. Remove the seeds. One of the halves is the head.

2 The oval slice of green pepper is the muzzle.

3 Place the muzzle on the head.

4 Place the two onion slices on the muzzle. These are the eyes.

5 Cut two rings from the green olive.

6 Cut two small rounds from the black olive.

7 Place the rounds on the green olive rings. These are the pupils. Place the pupils on the eyes.

8 Cut a red pepper ring in half. Cut off a small triangle from each end. Make three more such pieces. Two of them are the ears, one is the tail and one is for the whiskers.

9 Place the ears under the head. Place the whiskers under the muzzle. Use a black olive half for the nose.

10 Cut a light green pepper in half lengthwise. Cut one half again lengthwise.

11 Place one of the cut quarters against the head. This is the body.

12 Attach the tail to the body. Use the chive stalks for the legs.

13 Place beans against the legs. These are the paws.

Cat

INGREDIENTS

1 yellow pepper
1 green pepper
1 piece of red pepper
1 pitted green olive
2 pitted black olives
8 sweet peas
3 green stalks of chive
2 kidney beans
1 red chili pepper

1 Cut the yellow pepper in half lengthwise. One half is the head, the other is the body.

2 Cut the green pepper in half lengthwise. Remove the seeds. This is the mouth.

3 Cut one half again lengthwise. Place the head on the mouth, as shown.

4 Cut two rings from the green olive. These are the eyes.

5 Cut two small rounds from a black olive. These are the pupils.

6 Place the pupils on the eyes. Place the eyes on the head. Use the beans for the ears.

7 Cut a segment out of the black olive. The remainder of the olive is the nose.

8 Place the nose cut side down. Insert stalks of chive into the hole underneath. These are the whiskers.

9 Lay the nose and whiskers on the head. Place the body against the head.

10 Cut a red pepper ring in half. Cut off small triangles from the tips of each half.

11 These are the legs. Place them under the body.

12 Lay out paws using the sweet peas. Use a red chili pepper for the tail.

Cowboy

INGREDIENTS

1 yellow pepper
1 light green pepper
1 dark green pepper
1 red oblong pepper
3 pitted green olives
1 pitted black olive
2 chive stalks
2 kidney beans
1 red chili pepper
1 stalk of dill
1 red onion ring

1 Cut the yellow pepper in half lengthwise. Remove seeds from one half.

2 Cut the light green pepper in half lengthwise. Cut one half lengthwise again.

3 Put one fourth of the green pepper on the half of the yellow pepper. This is the head.

4 Cut the red oblong pepper into three pieces. The middle piece is the nose.

5 Place the nose on the head. Place the onion ring under the nose. This is the mouth.

6 Use two green olives for the eyes.

7 Cut two small rounds from the black olive. These are the pupils.

8 Place the pupils on the eyes. Insert a dill stalk as the hair.

9 Arrange the chili pepper as a hat brim. Use a square slice of red pepper for the top of the hat.

10 Place the full half of the light green pepper below the head. This is the body. Use two chive stalks for the arms.

11 Cut out legs from the dark green pepper.

12 Place the legs under the body. Use beans for the boots. Cut a green olive ring in half. These are the hands.

Hare

INGREDIENTS

1 light green pepper

1 dark green pepper

2 round slices of leek (from the bulb)

3 pitted green olives

2 pitted black olives

1 chive stalk

2 kidney beans

1 red chili pepper

4 corn kernels

1 Cut the light green pepper in half lengthwise.

2 Cut one half lengthwise again.

3 Lay out the two quarters as shown. This is the head.

4 Cut out ears from the dark green pepper.

5 Place the ears under the head.

6 The two leek slices are the eyes.

7 Cut two small rounds from a black olive. These are the pupils.

8 Place the pupils on the eyes. Place the eyes on the head.

9 Cut off a thin angled slice from a black olive.

10 Place the black olive cut side down under the eyes. This is the nose. Insert corn kernels into the mouth. These are the teeth.

11 Place the red chili pepper under the head. This is the body. Insert a chive stalk for the arms.

12 Use green olives for the hands.

13 Cut a ring from another green olive.

14 Cut this in half. These are the fingers. Place the fingers against the hands. Use the two beans as paws as shown.

Squirrel

INGREDIENTS

1 red pepper in as square a
   shape as possible

1 red oblong pepper

1 green pepper

1 red chili pepper

2 round slices of leek
   (from the bulb)

3 pitted green olives

3 pitted black olives

chive stalks

2 red onion rings

1 dill stalk

1 Cut a green pepper in
   half lengthwise.

2 Cut one half again
   lengthwise. Remove the
   seeds. Laid side by side,
   these are the head.

3 Cut the square
   red pepper in half
   lengthwise, preserving
   the stem on one half.

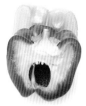

4 Place the pepper half with the stem on the head. This is the muzzle.

5 Cut out ears from the second red pepper half.

6 Place the ears against the head. Place the dill stalks at the tips of the ears.

7 Make a vertical incision in two of the green olives. These are the eyes.

8 Cut out a thin slice from a black olive. Cut one slice in two. These are the pupils.

9 Insert the pupils into the incisions in the eyes. Place the eyes on the head.

10 Attach a black olive to the red pepper stem. This is the nose. Place the leek slices on the muzzle. These are the cheeks. Place the chive stalks on the cheeks. These are the whiskers.

11 Cut a piece from the red oblong pepper. This is the body.

12 Cut two small pieces from one onion ring. Cut a second onion ring in half. These are the arms and feet.

13 Place the arms under and over the body, as shown. Lay out legs using the first onion half and the two smallpieces as feet. Use the red chili pepper for the tail.

14 Cut a black olive in half. Insert a dill stalk into it. Attach a green olive to complete the acorn. This is the acorn that the squirrel holds.

Meerkat

INGREDIENTS

1 red square pepper

1 red oblong pepper

1 green pepper

1 red chili pepper

2 round slices of red onion

2 pitted green olives

2 pitted black olives

2 corn kernels

4 kidney beans

1 Cut the square red pepper in half lengthwise. One of these is the head.

2 Cut the oblong pepper into three parts.

3 Lay the middle part on the head. This is the muzzle.

4 Cut ears from the second half of the red pepper.

5 Place the ears under the head.

6 Place a kidney bean on each onion slice. These are the eyelids.

7 Cut a green olive half in two. These are the eyes.

8 Cut tiny rounds from a black olive. These are the pupils.

9 Place the pupils on the eyes. Place the eyes under the eyelids. Place each complete eye on the head.

10 Make an incision in a green olive. This is the mouth.

11 Insert corn kernels into the incision. These are teeth.

12 Insert the mouth into the muzzle. Put half of a black olive on the muzzle. This is the nose.

13 Cut half of the light green pepper in half again lengthwise. One of the quarters is the body.

14 Lay the body next to the head. Use the beans as paws and the chili pepper as a tail.

Rooster

1 red pepper

1 yellow pepper

1 oblong red pepper

1 piece of green pepper

3 red onion rings

1 pitted black olive

2 round slices of leek
(from the bulb)

chive stalks

1 kidney bean

1 Cut the red pepper in half lengthwise.

2 One half is the head. Do not remove the seeds and flesh.

3 Cut the tip off the oblong red pepper. This is the beak.

40

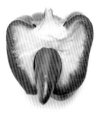

4 Insert the beak into hole in the head.

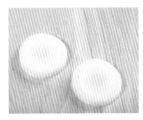

5 The two leek slices are the eyes.

6 Cut the bean in half. These are the pupils.

7 Place the pupils on the eyes. Place the eyes on the head.

8 Cut the yellow pepper in half lengthwise. This is the body.

9 Place the body next to the head.

10 Cut out wings from the green pepper piece.

11 Place the wings against the body. Use chive stalks for legs.

12 Cut a black olive ring in half. These are the claws.

13 Attach the paws to the legs.

14 Cut each onion ring in half. Lay out a tail.

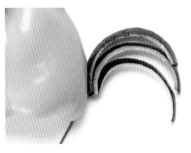

Moose

1 red pepper
1 yellow pepper
1 green pepper
1 pitted black olive
2 pitted green olives
chive stalks
parsley stalk
2 basil leaves
2 corn kernels

1 Cut the red pepper in half lengthwise. One half is the head.

2 Cut the green pepper in half. Cut one half lengthwise in two.

3 Arrange two of the quarters as shown. This is the muzzle. Insert two corn kernels inside the muzzle as shown. These are the teeth.

4 Place the muzzle under the head.

5 Cut a green olive half in two. These are the eyelids.

6 Cut two tiny rounds from the black olive These are the eyes.

7 Place the eyelids on the head. Place the eyes under the eyelids.

8 Cut two rings from a green olive.

9 Place them on the muzzle. These are the nostrils.

10 Use the basil leaves for the ears and parsley stalks for the antlers.

11 Cut a piece of yellow pepper. This is the body.

12 Place the body next to the head. Use chive stalks for the legs.

13 Cut the tip off the black olive.

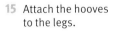

14 Cut this into four parts. These are the hooves.

15 Attach the hooves to the legs.

Monkey

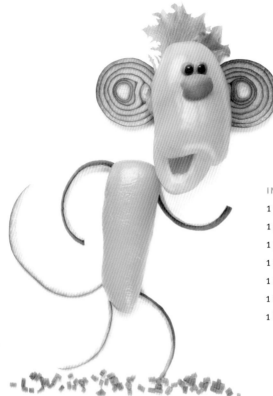

INGREDIENTS

1 yellow pepper
1 green pepper
1 pitted black olive
1 pitted green olive
1 red onion
1 sweet pea
1 lettuce leaf

1 Cut the yellow pepper in half lengthwise. Remove the seeds.

2 Cut one half in two pieces as shown. These are the preforms for the head.

3 Place the smaller piece cut side up. Place the lettuce leaf under the piece.

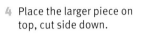

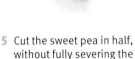

4 Place the larger piece on top, cut side down.

5 Cut the sweet pea in half, without fully severing the two halves.

6 Unfold the halves. These are the eyes.

7 Cut two tiny rounds from the black olive. These are the pupils.

8 Place the pupils on the eyes.

9 Place the eyes on the head. Use half of the green olive for the nose.

10 Use two round onion slices for the ears.

11 Cut the green pepper in half lengthwise. Cut one half lengthwise again. This is the body. Place next to the head.

12 Cut out onion rings to make legs, arms and a tail.

Horse

INGREDIENTS

1 red pepper

1 piece of green pepper

2 pitted black olives

2 pitted green olives

stalks of chive

2 red chili peppers

1 lettuce leaf

1 Cut the red pepper in half lengthwise.

2 Cut one half into two segments.

3 Put the smaller segment cut side up. This is the head. Put the larger segment cut side down over top. This is the muzzle.

4 Cut a tiny triangle from the second pepper half.

5 Place this under the muzzle. This is the mouth.

6 Cut a green olive in half, without fully severing the two halves. Unfold the olive halves. These are the eyes.

7 Cut two small rounds from a black olive. These are the pupils.

8 Place the pupils on the eyes. Lay the eyes on the head.

9 Cut two rings from the second green olive. These are the nostrils.

10 Cut ears out of the green pepper slice.

11 Lay out a lettuce leaf in the form of a mane. Place the ears against the head.

12 Use one red chili pepper for the neck. The second chili pepper is the body. Use chive stalks for legs.

13 Cut a black olive into quarters. These are the hooves.

14 Attach the hooves to the legs. Use another lettuce leaf for the tail.

Teacher

INGREDIENTS

1 red pepper

1 yellow pepper

1 oblong red pepper

1 piece of green pepper

2 pitted black olives

3 pitted green olives

1 lettuce leaf

2 red chili peppers

1 red onion

1 kidney bean

1 Cut a red pepper in half lengthwise.

2 Cut one half in two segments. Lay these side by side, cut sides up. This is the head. Lay out lettuce leaves in the form of a hairstyle.

3 Make a wide incision in each of two green olives but do not split them. These are the eyes. The black olives are the pupils.

4 Insert the pupils into the incision in the eyes. Place the eyes on the head. Use onion rings for eyeglasses.

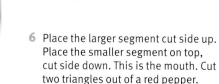

5 Cut a yellow pepper in half. Cut one half into two segments.

6 Place the larger segment cut side up. Place the smaller segment on top, cut side down. This is the mouth. Cut two triangles out of a red pepper. These are the lips.

7 Insert the lips into the mouth as shown.

8 Use a small piece of lettuce for the moustache. Cut out a nose from the remaining piece of yellow pepper.

9 Place the nose on the face. Use onion rings for the ears.

10 Cut the tip off of the oblong red pepper. This is the body.

11 Cut long strips out of the green pepper for the legs.

12 Arrange the body and legs. Use the chili peppers for the arms. Cut out hands from green olive halves. Cut the kidney bean in half lengthwise for the boots. Place them cut side down at the end of the legs.

Bee

INGREDIENTS

1 red pepper
1 yellow pepper
1 piece of green pepper
2 pitted black olives
1 pitted green olive
1 chive stalk

1 Cut off a segment from half of the red pepper.

2 Cut a similar-sized segment from the yellow pepper.

3 Cut both segments into strips.

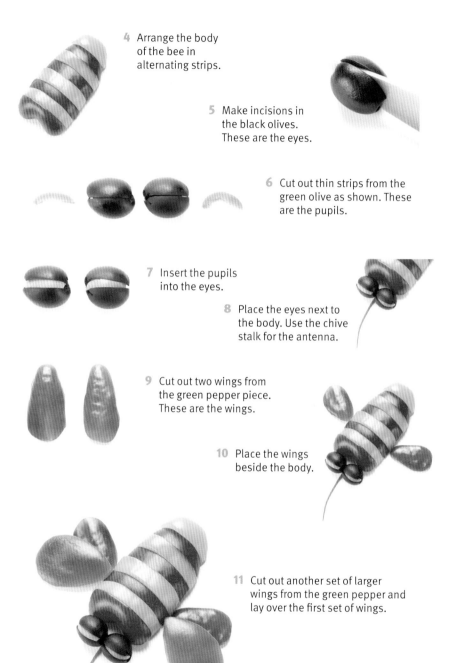

4 Arrange the body of the bee in alternating strips.

5 Make incisions in the black olives. These are the eyes.

6 Cut out thin strips from the green olive as shown. These are the pupils.

7 Insert the pupils into the eyes.

8 Place the eyes next to the body. Use the chive stalk for the antenna.

9 Cut out two wings from the green pepper piece. These are the wings.

10 Place the wings beside the body.

11 Cut out another set of larger wings from the green pepper and lay over the first set of wings.

Palm Tree

INGREDIENTS

1 oblong red pepper
1 green pepper
corn kernels

1 Make a vertical incision in the red pepper.

2 Cut out a segment as shown. This is the trunk of the palm tree.

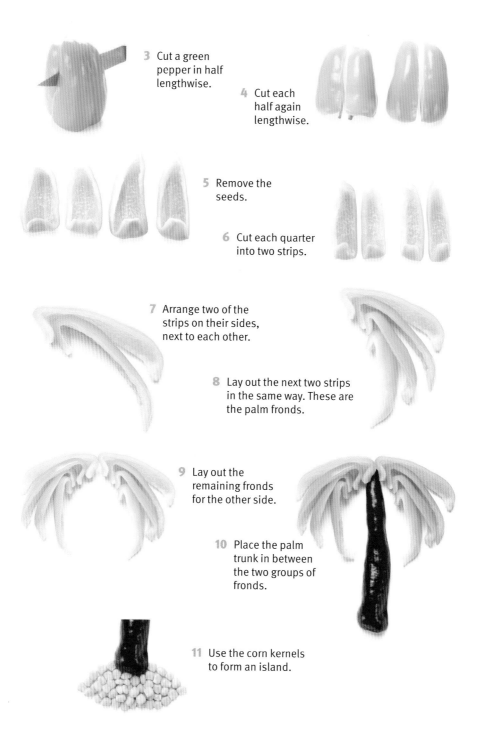

3 Cut a green pepper in half lengthwise.

4 Cut each half again lengthwise.

5 Remove the seeds.

6 Cut each quarter into two strips.

7 Arrange two of the strips on their sides, next to each other.

8 Lay out the next two strips in the same way. These are the palm fronds.

9 Lay out the remaining fronds for the other side.

10 Place the palm trunk in between the two groups of fronds.

11 Use the corn kernels to form an island.

Tiger

INGREDIENTS

1 red pepper
1 yellow pepper
3 pitted green olives
2 pitted black olives
1 kidney bean
green stalks of chive
sweet peas

1 Cut the yellow pepper in half lengthwise. One half is the head.

2 Cut the red pepper in half. Cut one half in two. Cut one of the quarters into strips.

3 Lay the strips in the head as shown.

4 Cut two small rounds from a black olive. These are the pupils.

5 Place the pupils on the green olives. These are the eyes.

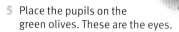

6 Insert chive stalks into a black olive. This is the nose and whiskers.

7 Place the nose on the muzzle.

8 Cut the bean in half lengthwise.

9 The bean is the mouth. Cut green olive halves for the ears.

10 Cut out identical pieces from the slices of red and yellow pepper.

11 Cut both slices into strips.

12 Lay out the tiger's body using alternating strips.

13 Use red strips for the legs and a yellow strip for the tail. Use peas to make the paws. You can also use peas to make a grass strip.

Spider

INGREDIENTS

1 red pepper
1 green pepper
1 yellow pepper
1 pitted black olive
2 sweet peas

1 Cut the green pepper in half lengthwise.

2 Cut each half into two quarters.

3 Remove the seeds.

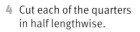

4 Cut each of the quarters in half lengthwise.

5 Lay one strip on its side.

6 Lay out another three strips next to the first one. These are legs.

7 Lay out another four legs for the other side.

8 Cut a segment from the yellow pepper. This is the head.

9 Cut the red pepper in half lengthwise.

10 This is the spider's body.

11 Cut off the tips from the black olive. Cut the middle part into two rings, without fully severing the two halves.

12 Unfold the halves. Place them on the head. These are the eyes. Insert the two peas as pupils.

Car

INGREDIENTS

1 red pepper
1 green pepper
1 yellow pepper
4 pitted black olives
2 pitted green olives

1 Cut a wide segment off the red pepper. This is the body of the car. Cut a narrow strip off the green pepper. This is the roof.

2 Attach the roof to the car body as shown.

3 Set the car body right side up.

4 Place the black olives against the car body. These are the wheels.

5 Cut a wide segment from the yellow pepper.

6 Cut a narrow piece from the segment. Slice the piece into narrow strips. The rounded tip is the cabin.

7 Choose four similarly-sized strips. These are the tire rims. Place them on the wheels.

8 Set the cabin on the car body.

9 Cut an oblique slice from each of the two green olives, leaving the hole in each uncut.

10 These are the headlights.

11 Attach the headlights to the car body.

Dragon

INGREDIENTS

1 red oblong pepper
2 pitted black olives
2 pitted green olives
1 red onion ring
2 basil leaves
corn kernels
1 kidney bean

1 Cut the pepper in half lengthwise.

2 Remove the seeds from one half.

3 Place this half cut side down. Make horizontal incisions along the top without cutting all the way through. Leave the small end unmarked. This is the body and head.

4 Bend the body. Insert a corn kernel into each incision. This is the spine.

5 Place a whole green olive next to the head. This is one eye.

6 Cut out a half from the second green olive. This is the second eye.

7 Place the second eye on the head.

8 Cut the tips off the bean. These are the pupils.

9 Place the pupils on the eyes.

10 Cut out the tail from the second half of the pepper.

11 Make arms from the onion ring.

12 Cut a black olive in half. These are the legs. Cut out claws and place next to body.

13 Attach the arms. Use basil leaves for the wings. Attach the tail.

Snail

INGREDIENTS

1 red oblong pepper

1 yellow pepper

1 pitted black olive

1 pitted green olive

2 round slices of red onion

1 sweet pea

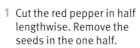

1 Cut the red pepper in half lengthwise. Remove the seeds in the one half.

2 Place the half cut side down. Make horizontal incisions along the pepper without cutting all the way through. Leave the small end untouched. This is the body and head.

3 Bend the body.

4 The two onions slices are the eyes.

5 Cut a green olive in half lengthwise. Cut one half in two. These are the eyelids.

6 Cut the tip off the black olive.

7 Cut this in half. These are the pupils.

8 Place the eyelids on the eyes.

9 Place the pupils under the eyelids. Place the eyes on the head.

10 The remaining green olive half is the mouth. Use the sweet pea for the nose.

11 Cut a yellow pepper in half lengthwise.

12 One half is the snail shell. Cut out tentacles from the second half.

Elephant

INGREDIENTS

1 red oblong pepper
1 red conical pepper
1 yellow pepper
1 light green pepper
1 piece of dark green pepper
1 pitted black olive
2 pitted green olives
6 corn kernels

1 Cut a narrow lengthwise segment from the red oblong pepper.

2 Place the segment cut side down. Make horizontal incisions across the top without cutting all the way through. This is the elephant's trunk.

3 Bend the turnk.

4 Cut the red pepper in half lengthwise. Place cut side up. This is the head. Attach the trunk.

5 Cut a strip out of the conical red pepper. Insert it into a green olive.

6 String a second green olive onto the pepper strip. These are the eyes.

7 Cut two small rounds from the black olive. These are the pupils.

8 Place the pupils on the eyes. Place the eyes on top of the head.

9 Cut out ears from the dark green pepper.

10 Place the ears under the head.

11 Cut the yellow pepper in half lengthwise. One half is the body.

12 Place the body next to the head. Cut out tusks from the yellow pepper.

13 Cut strips out of the light green pepper. These are the legs.

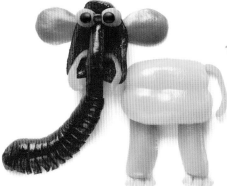

14 Place the legs under the body. Lay out corn kernels to the legs for the toes. Cut out a strip from the yellow pepper for the tail.

Porcupine

INGREDIENTS

1 red oblong pepper

1 green pepper

2 pitted black olives

1 pitted green olive

2 kidney beans

2 small slices of red onion

1 Cut a green pepper in half lengthwise.

2 Remove the seeds. Cut each half into quarters lengthwise.

3 Put one of the quarters at an angle cut side up. The pointed tip is the muzzle. Place a second quarter on top as shown.

4 Arrange two more quarters. This is the body.

5 Cut a red pepper in half lengthwise. Remove the seeds from one half.

6 Place the half cut side down. Make horizontal incisions along the entire length without cutting all the way through.

7 Turn over cut side up and bend as shown. These are needles of the porcupine.

8 Cut a tip of a black olive in half. These are the pupils.

9 One onion slice is an eye. Place a pupil on the eye.

10 Cut a green olive in half lengthwise. Cut each half into quarters. These are the eyelids.

11 Place the eyelids on the eye.

12 Make the second eye in the same way.

13 Attach a black olive to the muzzle for the nose. Use the beans for the legs.

Seahorse

INGREDIENTS

1 red oblong pepper
1 piece of green pepper
1 pitted black olive
1 pitted green olive
2 sweet peas
1 chili pepper

1 Cut the red pepper in half lengthwise. Remove the seeds from one half. This is the preform for the seahorse 's body.

2 Put the half cut side down. Make incisions along one third of the piece, without cutting all the way through and starting from the tip.

3 Cut incisions in the middle part of the preform from the opposite side. Do not cut all the way through.

4 Make incisions in the last third of the preform on the opposite side, being careful not to cut through the pepper.

5 Bend the preform. This is the body of the seahorse.

6 Place a chili pepper against the body. This is the head.

7 Cut a green olive in half, without fully severing the two halves.

8 Unfold the halves. These are the eyes. Insert the peas into the holes.

9 Cut two tiny rounds from the black olive. These are the pupils.

10 Place the pupils on the eyes. Place the eyes on the head.

11 Cut a small piece of green pepper. Place cut side down and make incisions in it. This is the fin.

12 Place the fin against the body.

Camel

INGREDIENTS

1 green pepper
1 piece of red pepper
2 pitted black olives
1 pitted green olive
1 corn kernel
2 round slices of red
   onion

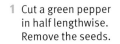

1 Cut a green pepper
   in half lengthwise.
   Remove the seeds.

2 Cut each half into
   quarters.

3 Cut each quarter in half
   lengthwise.

4 One strip is the head.

5 Cut two small rounds from a black olive These are the eyes. Place the eyes the head.

6 Cut a corn kernel in half lengthwise, without fully severing the two halves.

7 Unfold the corn halves. Place them on the eyes. These are the eyelids.

8 Make vertical incisions in two strips of green pepper, without fully severing. These are the legs.

9 Use one more strip for the body. Cut a thin strip out of this for the neck. Place the body on the legs. Place the neck against the body.

10 Attach the head. Use the green olive cut in half lengthwise for the ears.

11 Cut out lips from the piece of red pepper.

12 Cut the onion slice in half. These are the camel's humps.

13 Place the humps on the body. Place the lips under the muzzle.

14 Cut a black olive in half. Cut each half into quarters. These are the hooves. Attach the hooves to the legs.

Poppy

INGREDIENTS

1 long red pepper
1 green olive
red lettuce leaves
arugula leaves

1 Cut off the wide end of the pepper.

2 Remove the seeds.

3 Carve four petals around the stem.

4 Carefully slice each petal in two, separating the peel from the pulp with a sharp, narrow knife.

5 Refine the internal petals by trimming pulp from both sides, as shown. This is the preform for the poppy.

6 Put the preform in cold water for 20 minutes.

7 The external petals will curl out during this time.

8 Insert a small piece of lettuce inside the flower.

9 Insert a green olive in the center of the lettuce.

10 Make two more poppies and decorate with arugula leaves as shown above.

Red Lily

INGREDIENTS

1 long red pepper
1 green onion
parsley leaves
corn kernels

1 Cut a slice from the tip of the pepper. This is the preform for the flower. Cut out narrow sharp petals around the preform.

2 Cut narrow internal slices from the petals.

3 These are the stamens.

4 Cut out teeth on each petal.

5 Carefully cut each petal in two, separating the peel from the pulp with a knife.

6 Cut also each stamen lengthways in two.

7 Place the flower in cold water for 20 minutes. The external skin of petals will turn out during this time.

8 Cut the tip of the onion into strips. This is the stem.

9 You can also make one more short stem.

10 Join the lily to the stem.

11 Attach the short stem. Make another smaller lily.

12 Lay out a vase of corn kernels. Attach parsley leaves to the stem.

Yellow Flower

INGREDIENTS

1 yellow pepper
1 green pepper
1 red pepper
6 kidney beans

1 Cut out petals around the top of the yellow pepper.

2 Separate cut parts of the pepper.

3 Cut out internal membranes from the petals.

4 Cut off superfluous pulp at the edge of petals.

5 Cut out a hole in the center of the flower.

6 Cut a long narrow slice from the green pepper. Cut it in half. These are the preforms for leaves.

7 Cut out a leaf with a shaped edge.

8 Make an incision in the center of the leaf holding the knife at an angle. Change the angle of the knife and cut out a groove.

9 Cut short grooves on both sides in the same way. These are the veins.

10 Cut one more leaf in this way.

11 Cut a long strip off the remaining piece of pepper. This is the stem.

12 Attach the leaves to the stem. Lay the flower against the stem.

13 Cut out the middle section of the red pepper.

14 This is the vase. Insert the stem into the vase. Insert the beans into the center of the flower.

Daffodil

INGREDIENTS

1 yellow pepper
1 green pepper
1 red chili pepper

1 Cut out petals a round the
top of the yellow pepper.

2 Cut the internal
membranes from
the petals.

3 Carefully cut each
petal in two layers by
separating the peel
from the pulp with a
sharp narrow knife.

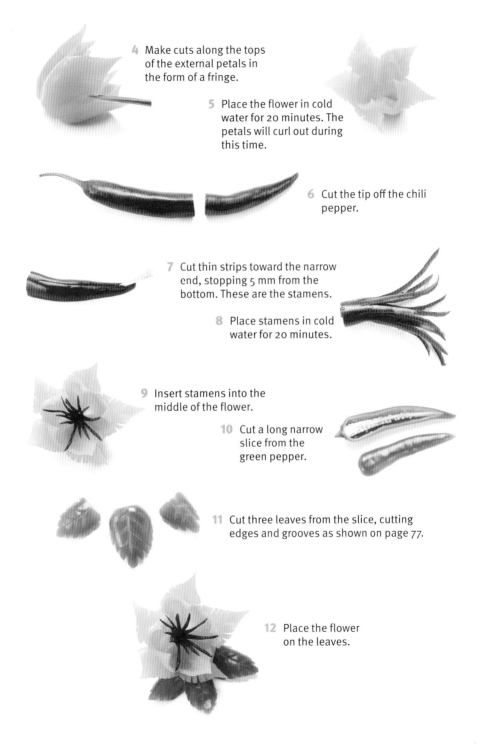

4 Make cuts along the tops of the external petals in the form of a fringe.

5 Place the flower in cold water for 20 minutes. The petals will curl out during this time.

6 Cut the tip off the chili pepper.

7 Cut thin strips toward the narrow end, stopping 5 mm from the bottom. These are the stamens.

8 Place stamens in cold water for 20 minutes.

9 Insert stamens into the middle of the flower.

10 Cut a long narrow slice from the green pepper.

11 Cut three leaves from the slice, cutting edges and grooves as shown on page 77.

12 Place the flower on the leaves.

Aster

INGREDIENTS

1 yellow pepper

2 green peppers

1 Cut a segment out of the yellow pepper as shown.

2 Cut two more segments. Remove the seeds. Cut out the stem.

3 Cut one segment in half horizontally.

4 Cut the halves into thin strips. These are the petals.

5 Choose the largest petals and arrange the bottom layer of petals.

6 Lay out the smaller petals on top.

7 Cut a long narrow slice from a green pepper. Cut this in half. These are the preforms for the leaves.

8 Cut out a leaf shape using a sharp knife.

9 Cut out a groove as shown using a thin narrow knife.

10 Cut short grooves on both sides in the same way. These are the veins.

11 Make one more leaf.

12 Cut a long strip from the remaining green pepper. This is the stem.

13 Cut the tip on an angle from the green pepper. This is the base of the flower.

14 Attach the stem to the flower. Place the base on top of the stem. Attach short stems and the leaves to the main stem.

Ginger Cat

INGREDIENTS

1 orange pepper
1 red pepper
2 pitted black olives
1 dill stalk

1 Cut a yellow or orange pepper in half lengthwise.

2 Remove the seeds and cut out the stem.

3 Cut the tip from one of the halves.

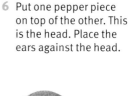

4 Cut this in two. These are the ears.

5 The two remaining parts of the pepper are part of the head.

6 Put one pepper piece on top of the other. This is the head. Place the ears against the head.

7 Cut two small rounds from a black olive. These are the eyes. Place the eyes on the head.

8 Cut out a slice from the second black olive. The large remaining piece is the nose.

9 Place the nose on the head. Insert fennel stalks in the hole for the whiskers.

10 Cut the stem end and the tip off the red pepper. The middle piece is the body. The tip is the tail.

11 Cut two rings from the middle part of pepper.

12 Cut each ring in two. These are the legs.

13 Attach the head to the body. Attach the tail and legs.

Exotic Flower

INGREDIENTS

1 green pepper

1 orange pepper

corn kernels

1 Use a long and narrow green pepper. Cut it into thin rings.

2 Lay out five rings in a circle. This is the outline of petals.

3 Put three more rings on top.

4 Cut four smaller rings in half.

5 Arrange the petal halves on top of each other in a checkered pattern.

6 Arrange the smallest petals at the top into a shallow peak.

7 Make two more flowers.

8 Create stems from the the corn kernels.

9 Cut out six small leaves from the orange pepper.

10 Place them next to the stems.

11 Cut out two bigger leaves from the orange pepper.

12 Place them at the base of the bouquet.

Fir

INGREDIENTS

1 green pepper
1 piece of orange pepper
corn kernels

1 Cut off the tip of a long green pepper at an angle.

2 This is the tree trunk.

3 Cut the remaining pepper into thin ovals. These are the branches.

4 Arrange these in order of size.

5 Lay out two big branches.

6 Put two more big branches on top of the first two.

7 Add branches of a smaller size.

8 Continue using successively smaller branches until you reach the tip.

9 Attach the trunk at the base of the tree.

10 Cut a moon out of a slice of the orange pepper.

11 Decorate the fir with corn kernels.

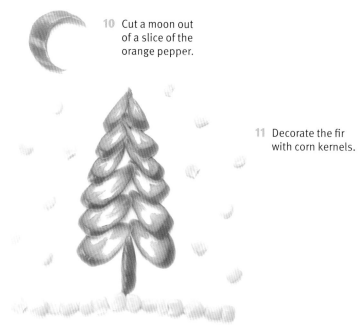

Poodle

INGREDIENTS

1 green pepper
1 piece of red pepper
2 pitted black olives
1 yellow pepper
1 corn kernel

1 Cut half of a long green pepper into thin rings.

2 The remaining half of the pepper is the head.

3 Attach a black olive to the stem on the head. This is the nose.

4 Cut the corn kernel in half lengthwise, without completely severing the two halves. Unfold the halves. These are the eyes.

5 Cut tiny rounds from the other black olive. These are the pupils.

6 Place the pupils on the eyes.

7 Place the eyes on the head. Lay out ears and hair using the pepper rings.

8 Cut out a bow from the red pepper.

9 Place the bow on the head. Use more pepper rings to make the neck.

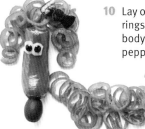

10 Lay out the remaining rings in the shape of the body. Use one half of a pepper ring for the tail.

11 Cut a segment from the yellow pepper.

12 Cut the segment in half. Cut this into four strips. These are the legs.

13 Attach the legs to the body.

Crab

INGREDIENTS

1 orange pepper
2 pitted black olives
2 round slices of red onion
1 piece of red pepper
4 corn kernels

1 Cut an orange pepper in half horizontally.

2 Remove the seeds and cut out the internal membranes from both halves.

3 Place the bottom half cut side down. This is the body. Cut out holes for the eyes using an apple corer.

4 Make an incision for the mouth.

5 Insert corn kernels into the incision. These are the teeth. Insert black olives into the holes. These are the eyes.

6 Separate the rings in each onion slice.

7 Place an onion ring on each eye.

8 Cut two rings from the top half of the pepper.

9 Make a cut in one of them. These are the forelegs.

10 Cut the second ring into six slices. These are the hind legs.

11 Arrange the legs as shown.

12 Place the body on top of the legs.

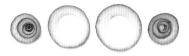

13 Cut two angled pieces from the tip of the red pepper.

14 Make a cut in the narrow part of each piece. These are the claws.

Frog

1 Cut out a wide segment lengthwise from the green pepper. This is the body.

2 Cut one more segment off the pepper and remove the seeds.

3 Cut a circular arc from the narrow tip of the segment. This is the mouth.

4 Cut out the hind legs from this segment.

5 Cut out the forelegs from the remaining part of this segment.

6 Place the mouth under the head. Place the legs against the body.

7 Cut the tips off the green olive. Cut the middle part into rings, without fully severing the two halves. These are the eyes.

8 Cut one olive tip in half. These are the eyelids.

9 Place the eyelids on the eyes.

10 Cut side slices from half of the black olive. These are the pupils.

11 Place the pupils on the eyes. Place the eyes on the head.

12 Cut out a tongue from the red pepper.

13 Insert the tongue into the mouth. Use the sweet peas for the toes.

Daisy

INGREDIENTS

1 orange pepper
1 parsley stalk
1 piece of red pepper

1 Cut out petals around the wide end of the orange pepper.

2 Separate the flower from the rest of the pepper.

3 Remove the seeds.

4 Turn up the flower and unfold the petals.

5 Use the parsley stalk as the stem.

6 Place the stem next to the flower.

7 Cut the tip off the red pepper. The remaining piece is the vase.

8 Insert the stem into the vase.

9 You can also make a bouquet of daisies.

10 Cut thin ovals from a green pepper.

11 Lay out the ovals in form of leaves.

12 Cut strips out of a green pepper for the stems.

A FIREFLY BOOK

Published by Firefly Books Ltd. 2016

First printing

PUBLISHER CATALOGING-IN-PUBLICATION DATA (U.S.)
Names: Stepanova, Iryna, author. | Kabachenko, Sergiy, author.
Title: Pepper creatures : make your own / Iryna Stepanova, Sergiy Kabachenko.
Description: Richmond Hill, Ontario, Canada : Firefly Books, 2016. | Series: Make Your Own | Summary: Food presentation skills for cooks, chefs, and parents are provided with step by step instructions and photographs of each step.
Identifiers: ISBN 978-1-77085-855-8 (hardcover)
Subjects: LCSH: Cooking (Peppers). | Food presentation. | Garnishes (Cooking)
Classification: LCC TX740.5S747 |DDC 641.819 – dc23

LIBRARY AND ARCHIVES CANADA CATALOGUING IN PUBLICATION
Stepanova, Iryna, author
Pepper creatures : make your own / Iryna Stepanova and Sergiy Kabachenko.
(Make your own ; 3)
ISBN 978-1-77085-855-8 (hardback)
1. Food craft. 2. Food presentation. 3. Cooking (Garnishes).
4. Cooking (Peppers). I. Kabachenko, Sergiy, author II. Title.
TX740.5.S76 2016   745.5   C2016-903718-5

Published in the United States by
Firefly Books (U.S.) Inc.
P.O. Box 1338, Ellicott Station
Buffalo, New York 14205

Published in Canada by
Firefly Books Ltd.
50 Staples Avenue, Unit 1
Richmond Hill, Ontario L4B 0A7

Cover and interior design: Peter Ross / Counterpunch Inc.

Printed in China

The publisher gratefully acknowledges the financial support for our publishing program by the Government of Canada through the Canada Book Fund as administered by the Department of Canadian Heritage.